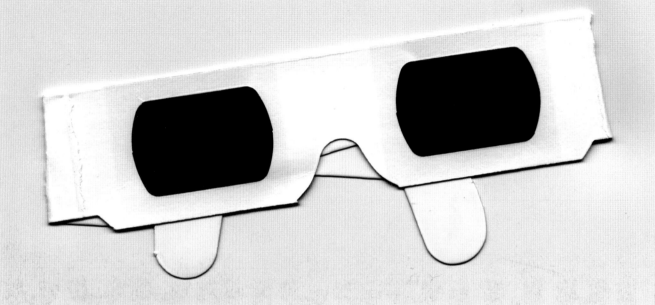

flatnessisgod

art + design + process + picture plane theory + x,y

Ryan McGinness

flatnessisgod

flatnessisgod
art + design + process + picture plane theory + x,y
Ryan McGinness.

Published by Soft Skull Press and
Razorfish Studios in New York City.

www.razorfishstudios.com
www.softskull.com

Art + Design + Words © 1999 Ryan McGinness.
ryanmcg@interport.net

Carah von Funk and Lisa Shimamura
Production Managers

Michael Simon & Craig Kanarick
Chief Executives, Production

Jeff Dachis
Executive Producer

Sander Hicks
Editor

flatnessisgod limited-edition CD ROM
Ryan McGinness
Stephen Turbek
Marina Zurkow

Distributed in North America
by Consortium Book Sales and Distribution
St. Paul, Minnesota

First published in the United States of America in 1999.
Printed and bound in USA
First Edition of 4,500, April 1999

ISBN 1.887128.34.4

Publishing Information.
Cataloging. Copyrighting. Formats and standards.
This book is just part of the larger picture.

International Standard Book Number.

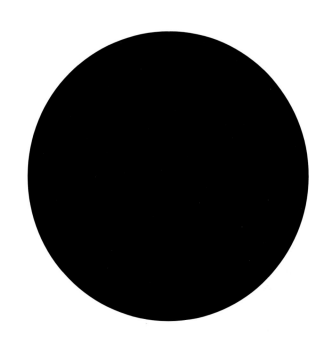

27.8 x 21.5 cm. Ink on paper.

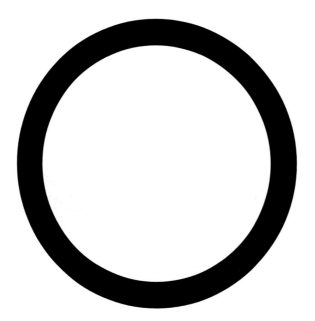

Lorem ipsum dolor sit amet, consectetuer adipiscing elit, sed diam nonummy nibh euismod tincidunt ut laoreet dolore magna aliquam erat volutpat. Ut wisi enim ad minim veniam, quis nostrud exerci tation ullamcorper suscipit lobortis nisl ut aliquip ex ea commodo consequat.
Duis autem vel eum iriure dolor in hendrerit in vulputate velit esse molestie consequat, vel illum dolore eu feugiat nulla facilisis at vero eros et accumsan et iusto odio dignissim qui blandit praesent luptatum zzril delenit augue duis dolore te feugait nulla facilisi. Lorem ipsum dolor sit amet, consectetuer adipiscing elit, sed diam nonummy nibh euismod tincidunt ut laoreet dolore magna aliquam erat volutpat.
Ut wisi enim ad minim veniam, quis nostrud exerci tation ullamcorper suscipit lobortis nisl ut aliquip ex ea commodo consequat. Duis autem vel eum iriure dolor in hendrerit

in vulputate velit esse molestie consequat, vel illum dolore eu feugiat nulla facilisis at vero eros et accumsan et iusto odio dignissim qui blandit praesent luptatum zzril delenit augue duis dolore te feugait nulla facilisi.
Nam liber tempor cum soluta nobis eleifend option congue nihil imperdiet doming id quod mazim placerat facer possim assum. Lorem ipsum dolor sit amet, consectetuer adipiscing elit, sed diam nonummy nibh euismod tincidunt ut laoreet dolore magna aliquam erat volutpat. Ut wisi enim ad minim veniam, quis nostrud exerci tation ullamcorper suscipit lobortis nisl ut aliquip ex ea commodo consequat. Duis autem vel eum iriure dolor in hendrerit in vulputate velit esse molestie consequat, vel illum dolore eu feugiat nulla facilisis. Lorem ipsum dolor sit amet, consectetuer adipiscing elit, sed diam nonummy nibh.

Letters. Symbols. Words. Fake text. Stand-in. Dummy text. Stupid symbols. These hold the place for the real.

This introduction is a symbol for an introduction. These words represent other words.

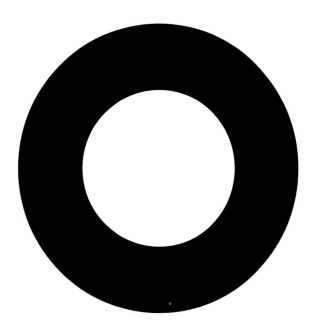

flatnessisgod ~~presents a original look at~~ ~~the~~ reading of the picture plane, ~~the~~ ~~domain of what exists~~ within an identity pastiche ~~of what is experienced and pro-~~ ~~ceived on the surface as a~~ symbol ~~or~~ ~~any other than an~~ object or idea. ~~In~~ ~~this way, he elaborates about how a~~ optic unconscious ~~pushing at the surface~~ possibilities. ~~The many effects that~~ ~~push the surface a~~ mainstream co-opts ~~overt graffiti marks as~~ signifiers ~~of a~~ ~~scrap of the interactions have with~~ x and y axis. ~~On the~~ ~~other, the experiments to~~ public domain identity codes ~~within a~~ ~~system. Both irony and heroism, a~~ genuine effort to understand ~~what we~~ ~~are being taught. Explores the~~ truth ~~and~~ surface integrity ~~within~~ systems. ~~By~~ ~~viewing through the~~ belief system ~~as it~~ ~~teaches us~~ how to interpret

images and shapes ~~based on ideas and~~ ~~appropriating~~ graffiti marks ~~these can for~~ ~~ground the but should be~~ original sight. ~~Furthermore, the preliminary~~ sketches ~~in~~ reveal a process ~~of experimentation that~~ ~~leads to~~ Where do solutions come from? Language ~~is the crux of what we do~~ ~~and how it comes to be and~~ viewed. ~~In~~ ~~this way the reader is inspired to repost~~ ~~and the~~ role of the visual communicator ~~by~~ ~~asking about a between art and~~ ~~design where do these end~~ experiments ~~with the process.~~ Questioning ~~where it comes from investigations~~ ~~of language pulled from the street~~ translations ~~and remixing and~~ subverting corporate ~~forms. From a~~ basic ~~design~~ ~~study to presenting~~ options ~~and across~~ ~~the picture, our text takes the~~ reader through ~~a series of steps by~~ recontextualizing ~~the ideas.~~

Introduction.

Reconsider.
Reconstruct what is given to you.

Edit. Distill.
Flatten.

005

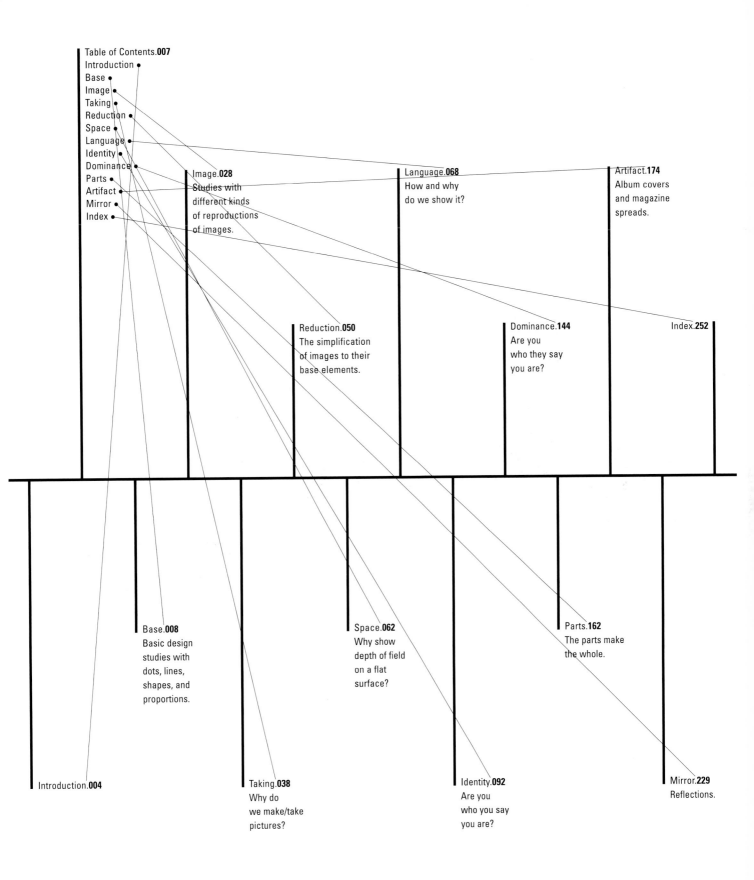

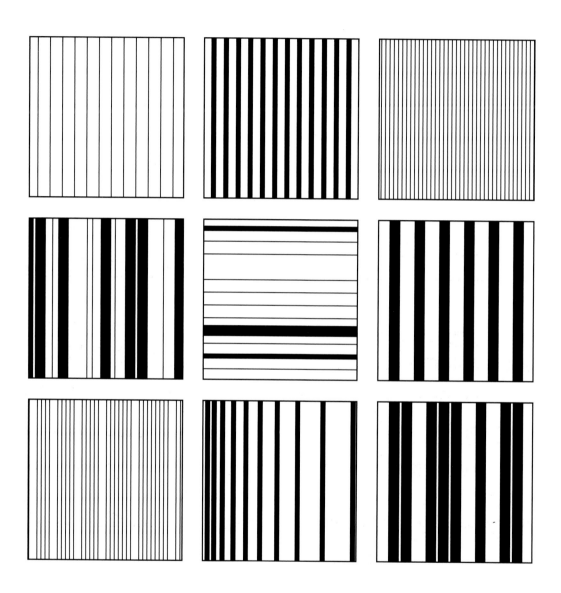

Base.

Line studies.
Variations on weight and spacing.

Vertical. Horizontal. Mechanical.

Base.

Line studies.
Variations on weight, spacing, length, and direction.

Mechanical. Hand-drawn. Machine. Human.
Cold. Warm. Formal. Casual. (See page 083.)

009

Base.

Line studies.
Variations on line width and spacing.

Actual size: 50 x 50 m. (See page 062.)
White/black lines on a black/white field.

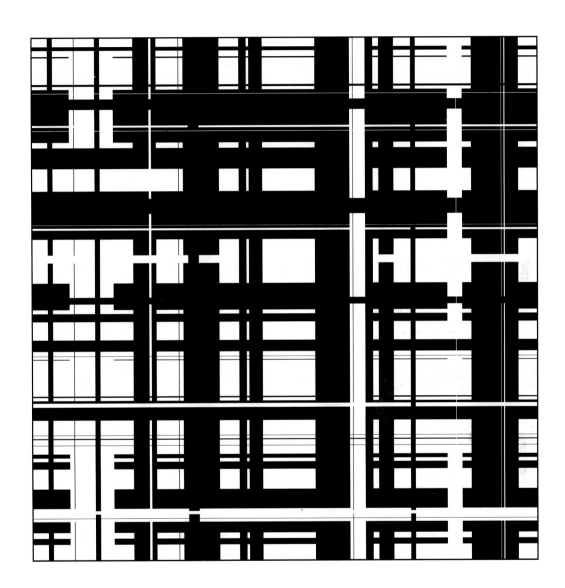

Base.

Line studies.
Black and white. Shapes.

Background. Foreground. In front. Behind.
Interruption. (See page 035.)

011

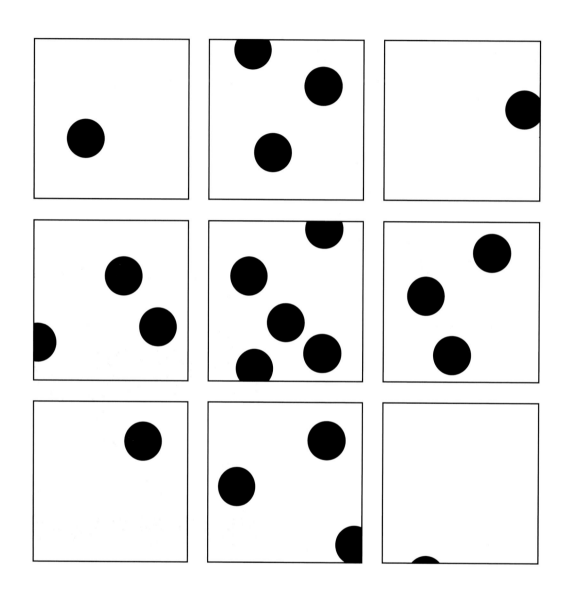

Base.

Dot studies.
Out of sight. Out of mind.

In the above 9 squares, 21 dots can be counted.
There are actually 25 dots. (See page 090.)

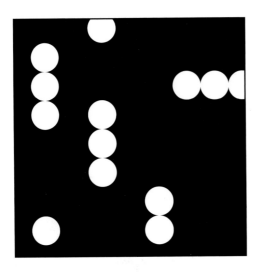
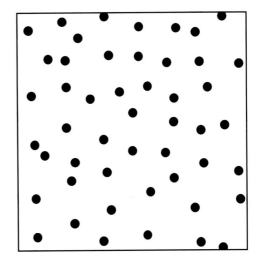
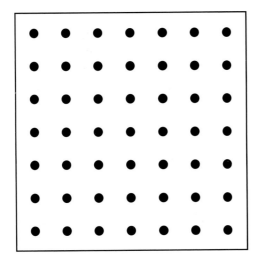
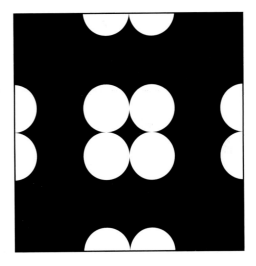

Base.

Dot studies.
Random. Ordered. A structure. A system.

Finite. Infinite space. Within. Beyond.
Implied motion. (See page 032.)

013

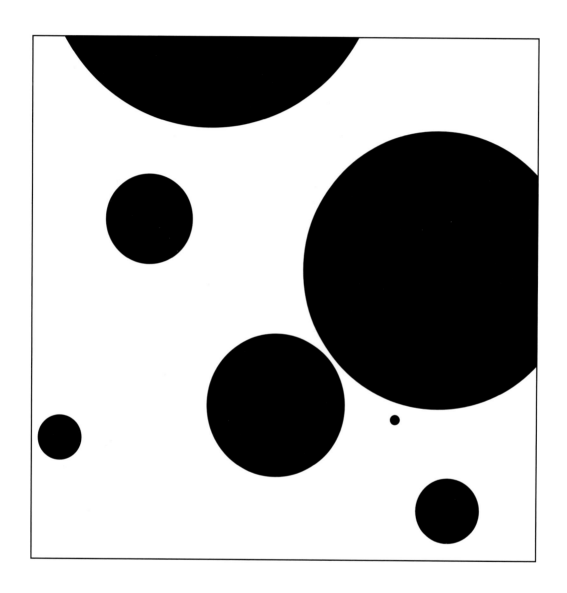

Base.

Dot studies.
Variations on weight and spacing.

Scale. Depth. Tension.
Space. (See page 061.)

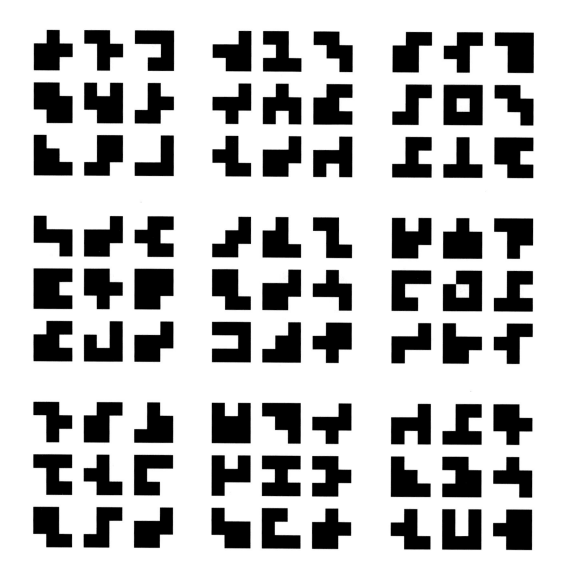

Base.

Shape studies.
Variations based on a system of squares.

3x3/3x3/3x3.
Flow between forms.

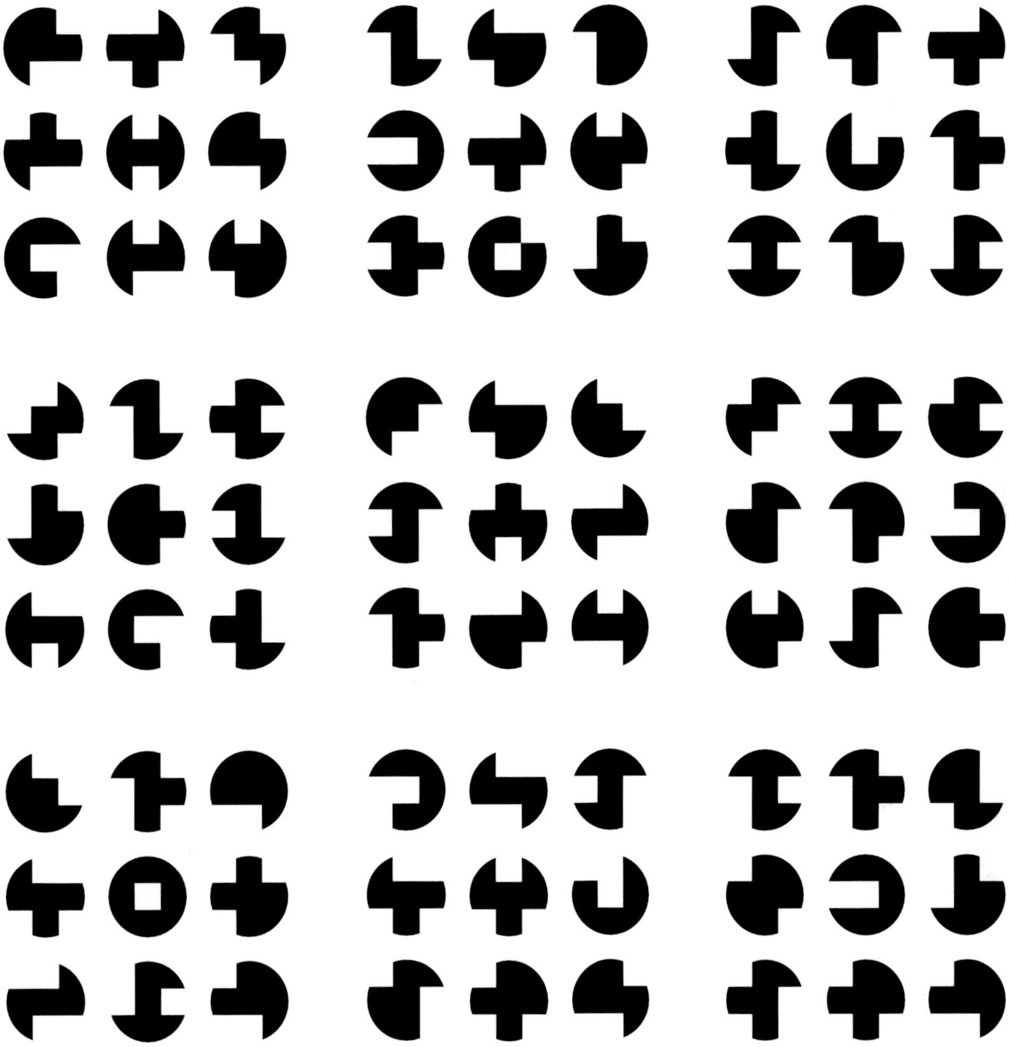

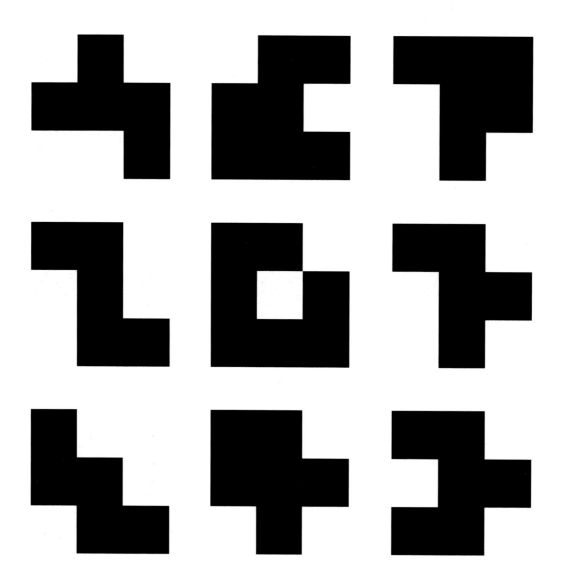

Base.
Shape studies.
Variations based on a system of squares.

3x3/3x3.

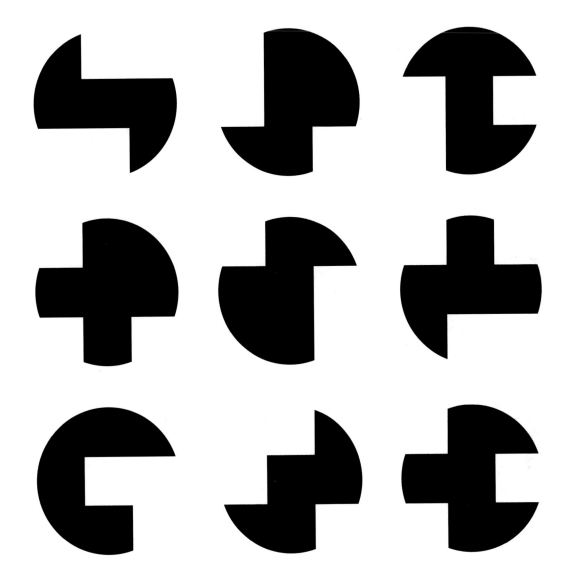

Base.

Shape studies.
One thing or three things? (See page 029.)

Positive. Negative.
White shapes on a black field.

Base.

Proportion studies.
Variations on horizontal and vertical divisions.

Structure.
Divisions within divisions. (See page 226.)

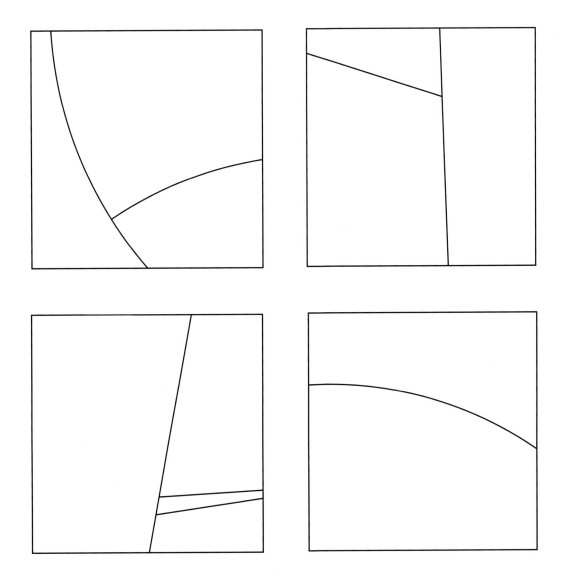

Base.

Proportion studies.
Areas of different values.

Hierarchy. By size, a value assignment.
Windows. (See page 026.)

Base.

Proportion studies.

The division of the picture plane can create
the illusion of space. Go into the field. (See page 066.)

025

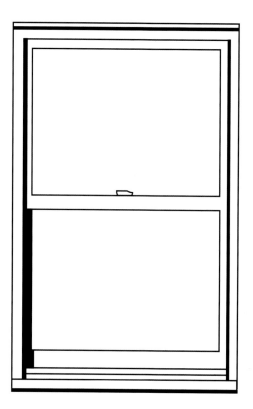

Base.

Windows. Frames.
Window frames.

Transparent or opaque? Picture portals. Containers.
Reveal or present?

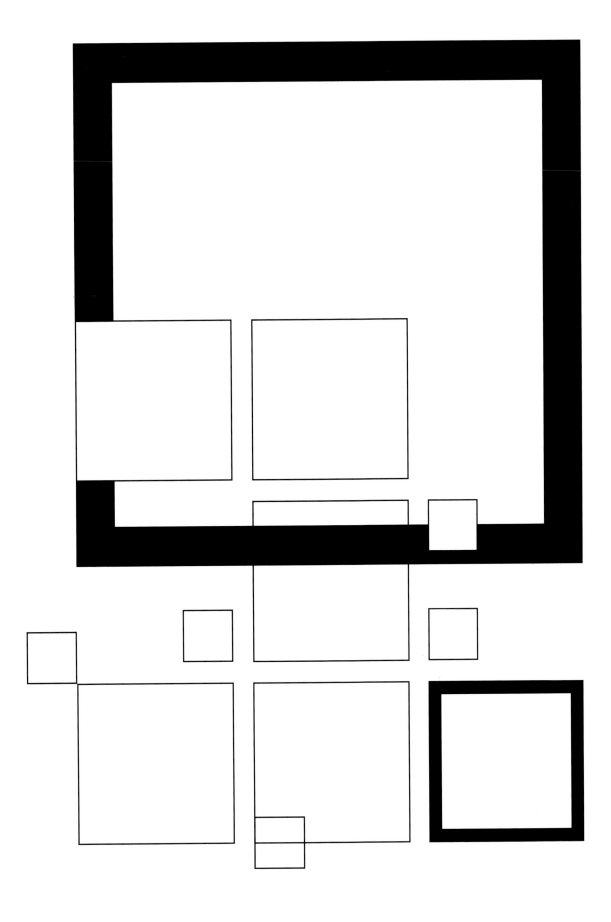

Image.

Picture taking. (See page 038.)
Signal sending.

(Re)productions of images. (See page 239.)

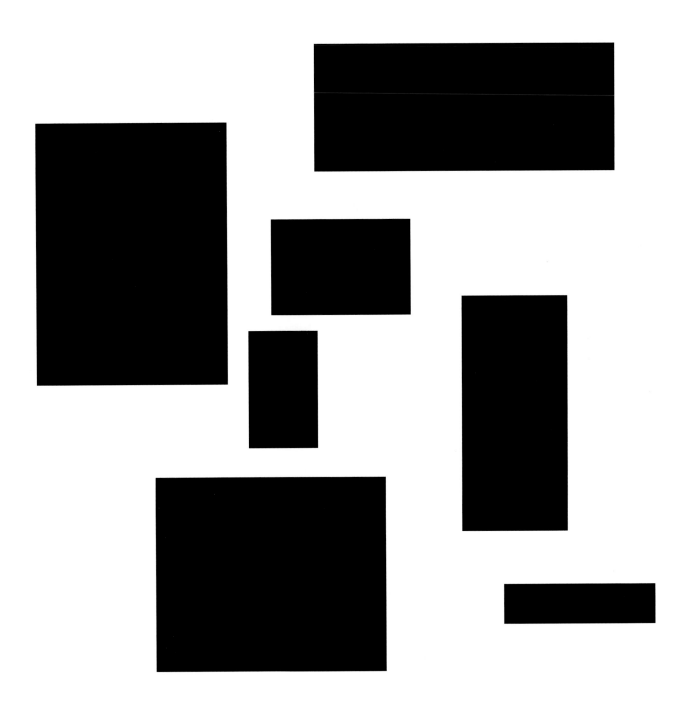

Image.

Things.
These things exist only on this page.

Subject matters.

029

Image.

Pictures of things.
The scissors are as large as the plane.

The (original) pictures and the things the pictures
are of exist elsewhere.

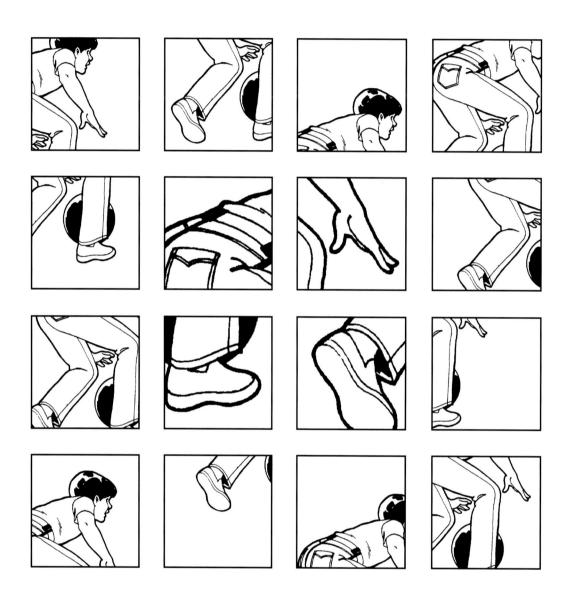

Image.

Within windows.
Variations on scale and cropping.

Direction and movement.
Elapsed time? Is there 1 boy or 16?

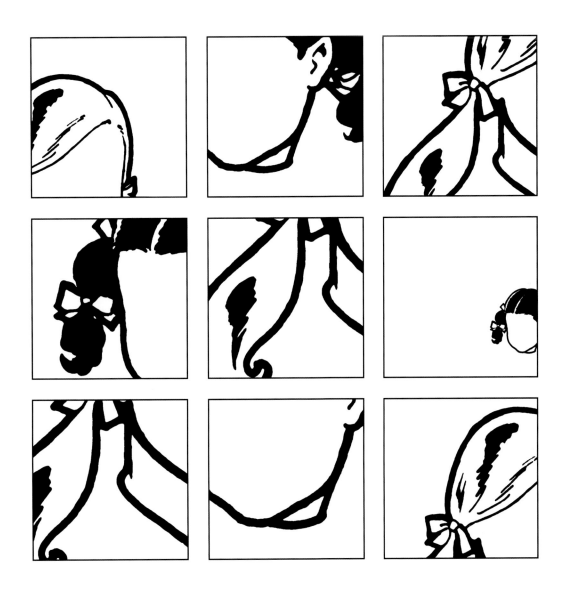

Image.

Parts. (See page 168.)
Scale and cropping.

Image transplant. Manipulation.
Anonymous.

033

Image.

Lines belong to forms.
Forms are transparent/opaque.

The images exist in/on the same field.
Multiple exposures.

Image.

Reproduction. Interruption. Scale.
Addition. Dot study. (See page 014.)

Elsewhere: 62 x 62 cm. Oil on canvas.
Here: 13.9 x 13.9 cm. Ink on paper.

Image.

Kinds of images.
Windows. Layers? What is behind? In front?

Context. History. Imposed narrative.
Here and now. (See page 031.)

Image.

Fragmentation. (See page 146.)
Surface interruption. Which surface?

Texture. Perceived texture. Image interruption.
122 x 122 cm. Oil and paper plates on canvas.

037

Taking.

Do you see what I see?
Do you see what he/she/they see?

Gender perspective. (See page 085.)
Looking.

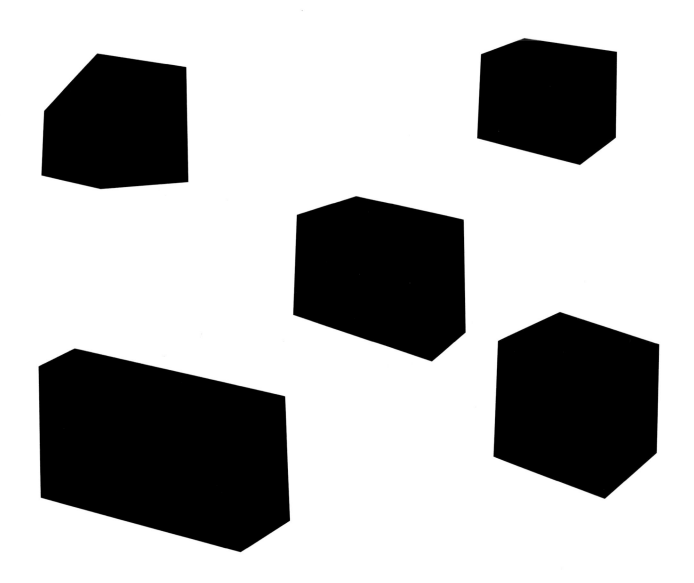

Taking.

Depictions of objects.
Shading. Lighting.

Boxes. Storage. Containers. (See page 050.)

Taking.

Forcing the third dimension into the second.
Making memories. Storing time.

Framing.
Flattening.

041

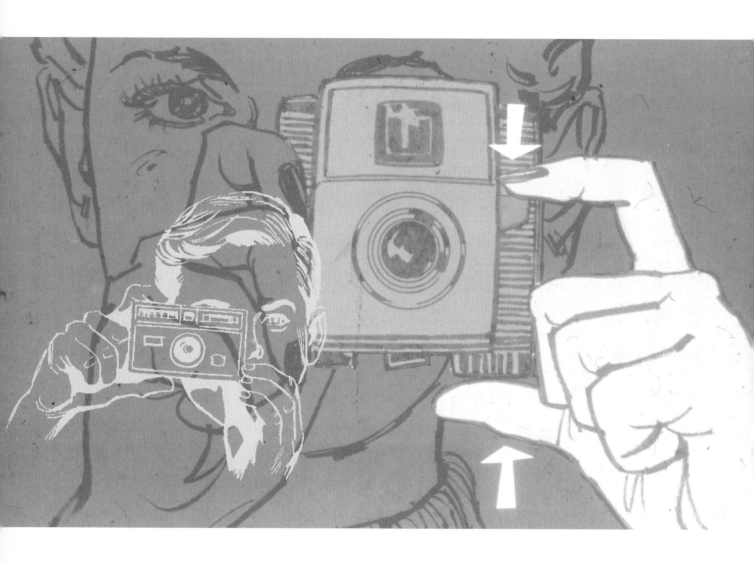

Taking.

A picture of you! Shoot. Capture. Document.
Looking through/making windows. Framing.

(Re)present. (Re)locate. You acknowledge the
grammar for looking at and making pictures.

KEEP AN AUDIENCE IN MIND